*Letters
to
Matthew*

Find Your Life's Passion

Don't lead a half-life, Matthew. I'm trying to help you find your passion. When you find your passion you'll never work again. Of course, you'll probably work extremely hard, but it won't seem like work. Because it is your passion, your purpose, your reason for being here.

A MYSTERIOUS SERIES of letters to Matthew from his former history teacher Mr. Nevin are the backbone of this inspirational book. The first letter from Mr. Nevin arrives just as the problems in Matthew's personal and business life are reaching a crisis level. Each well-timed letter gives Matthew encouragement and new ways to deal with his life.

After the seventh letter, Matthew sets out to find Mr. Nevin and thank him personally. As the story ends, Matthew discovers that the letters from Mr. Nevin truly are an extraordinary gift.

About the Author

Richard Webster was born in New Zealand in 1946, where he still resides. He travels widely every year, lecturing and conducting workshops on psychic subjects around the world. He has written many books, mainly on psychic subjects, and also writes monthly magazine columns. Richard is married with three children. His family is very supportive of his occupation, but his oldest son, after watching his father's career, has decided to become an accountant.

Many of Llewellyn's authors have websites with additional information and resources. For more information, please visit our website at www.llewellyn.com.

RICHARD WEBSTER

SUCCESS SECRETS

Letters

to

Matthew

2001
Llewellyn Publications
St. Paul, Minnesota 55164-0383, U.S.A.

First Edition
First Printing, 2001

Book design and editing by Michael Maupin
Cover design by Lisa Novak
Cover photo © Photodisk

Library of Congress Cataloging-in-Publication Data

Webster, Richard, 1946–
    Success secrets : letters to Matthew / Richard Webster.
        p.   cm.
    ISBN 1-56718-788-9
    1. Success. I. Title.

BJ1611.2.W393 2001
158.1—dc21   00-054970

Llewellyn Worldwide does not participate in, endorse, or have any authority or responsibility concerning private business transactions between our authors and the public.
    All mail addressed to the author is forwarded but the publisher cannot, unless specifically instructed by the author, give out an address or phone number.
    Any Internet references contained in this work are current at publication time, but the publisher cannot guarantee that a specific location will continue to be maintained. Please refer to the publisher's website for links to authors' websites and other sources.

Llewellyn Publications
A Division of Llewellyn Worldwide, Ltd.
P.O. Box 64383, Dept. 1-56718-788-9
St. Paul, MN 55164-0383, U.S.A.
www.llewellyn.com

Printed in the United States of America

Other Books by Richard Webster

Astral Travel for Beginners
Aura Reading for Beginners
Dowsing for Beginners
Feng Shui for Beginners
Llewellyn Feng Shui series
Numerology Magic
Omens, Oghams & Oracles
101 Feng Shui Tips for the Home
Palm Reading for Beginners
Seven Secrets to Success
Soul Mates
Spirit Guides and Angel Guardians

Forthcoming

Practical Guide to Past-Life Memories
Write Your Own Magic

For William,
our grandson

Dear Matthew

Chapter One

MATTHEW COLLAPSED into the chair behind his desk and closed his eyes. It was three-thirty. Normally, he would not be back in the office until at least four-thirty, but the day had been terrible. Rejections, delays, frustrations, and a few small orders. Sometimes he wondered why he kept on doing it.

The door to the sales office opened and Duncan came in, pale and stooped. He grunted at Matthew and slumped down in his chair.

"Your day must've been as bad as mine," Matthew said.

Duncan glanced at him. "Impossible," he said. "Mine was worse. A thousand times worse. I lost the Lochiel account."

Matthew sat bolt upright in his chair. Lochiel was Brazier Corporation's biggest customer, and everyone envied Duncan having them as his main account. "No," he said. "You couldn't have!" He looked at the expression on Duncan's face. "You did. You really lost them."

Duncan nodded. "Who'd have guessed that Roger Stacpole would be such a jerk? I was late—an hour and a half late, actually—for our appointment." Duncan rubbed his forehead wearily. "I tried to phone him but couldn't get through. I should have left a message, but I thought he'd understand. He's normally so laid back and calm."

"What did he do?"

"By the time I got there he'd given the order to Carter's. He's told them they can have the account for three months. How will I tell Wilbur?" Duncan sighed and shook his head. He looked at Matthew. "How was your day?"

Matthew smiled. "Not too bad, after all. Would you like me to go with you to tell Wilbur?"

Duncan shook his head. "Thanks, but I'd best do it on my own. I have to do it sometime. Might as well be now."

He got to his feet and went down the hall to Wilbur Aspac's office. Matthew could imagine the expression on the sales manager's face when he heard the news.

Wilbur was a gentle, soft-spoken man who avoided confrontation. Now, he'd have to visit Lochiel to see if the problem could be resolved. He'd have to sit meekly and let Roger Stacpole vent his spleen. But it would be worth it, Matthew thought. The Lochiel account was worth a hundred thousand a year. What if they didn't get it back? Would Wilbur's job be at stake? It wasn't his fault that Duncan had messed up, but he was the sales manager. It was his responsibility.

Matthew sighed and ran his fingers through his hair. It showed that no matter how many problems you had, other people had more. However, every day seemed to be getting worse and worse. He was virtually dragging himself around to call on his customers. He delayed answering phone calls and emails. What was the matter with him? His father had spent almost fifty years as a salesman and had loved every minute of it.

Maybe it was time he found another job. But hours of thinking had failed to produce anything else he could do. He couldn't resign without finding something else first. It wouldn't be so bad if Jennie had a job, but with the two boys at school and a mortgage to meet, they'd be in trouble in no time.

Matthew rolled his shoulders in an attempt to ease the stress that gathered in his upper back. *Think positive,* he told himself. *Keep away from negative thoughts.* He smiled as he recalled the words Wilbur Aspac regularly delivered to his sales staff. "If you find yourself thinking a negative thought, switch it around and make it positive." It was easy to say; not quite so easy to do.

The door opened slowly and Sam Milligan poked his head around the door and smiled nervously.

"Hi there, Matthew," he said.

"Welcome, Sam. You're back early, too. Has it been a hard day?" Sam scuttled nervously across the room to his desk.

Matthew watched him, aware that he made Sam even more self-conscious. Sam had been one of Wilbur's successes. He'd been promoted from the warehouse into sales, and despite his timidity had proven to be an excellent sales representative. His area, the northeast, had increased markedly over the ten months that Sam had looked after it.

Matthew's father had always claimed that only extroverts made good salespeople. Sam was well on the way to being the company's top salesman, and he was the most nervous man Matthew had ever met. Matthew watched him open his briefcase and pull out a pile of orders.

"Looks like you've had a good day," he observed.

Sam looked up briefly. "Yes, yes. Thanks." He carefully placed the orders on his immaculate desk and picked up a pen. "Oh, Matthew?" He licked his lips and his eyes did a circuit of the room before briefly meeting Matthew's. "Could I ask you for some advice?"

Matthew leaned back in his chair and nodded. "Sure. I'm flattered."

"Good, thanks. I appreciate it." Sam's Adam's apple bobbed up and down a few times. "I'm leaving," he said. "I've been offered another job. Do you think I should take it?"

Matthew's eyes widened. "Is it a good opportunity?"

Gradually, Matthew learned that Sam had been offered a key position in a startup company. He'd be a part-owner, and the opportunities seemed limitless.

"If someone offered me an opportunity like that," Matthew said. "You wouldn't see me for dust."

Sam shuffled his feet and scratched his nose. "Thank you. That's what I think. Now, how can I tell Wilbur?"

Duncan returned before Matthew could answer the question. He grabbed his coat and left, without acknowledging Sam's greeting. Matthew quickly explained what had happened.

"I've been putting off speaking to Wilbur," Sam said. "Just my luck that I have to do it today."

Matthew quickly wrote up his orders and took them to Avril, Wilbur's secretary. She was a pert, slim woman in her midtwenties. Her usual smile had been replaced with a frown.

"Cheer up," Matthew told her. *Look who's talking,* he told himself.

"Wilbur wants to see you," Avril said.

"Now?"

She nodded.

"Isn't Sam in there with him?"

"He was until a few minutes ago. He's free now."

Wilbur was studying a computer printout. He gestured to Matthew to sit down while he finished reading it. He put the report down on his desk with a sigh.

"I guess you've heard the news?" he said.

Matthew nodded. "About Lochiel? Yes." It didn't seem to be enough. Wilbur waited for more. "And about Sam. I'm sorry he's leaving."

Wilbur shook his head sadly. The round, innocent face beneath the long, wavy, out-of-control gray hair looked immensely sad.

"We'll all have to work a bit harder," Matthew said.

Wilbur picked up the computer printout and dropped it back onto his desk. "More than a bit," he said. His kindly eyes had lost their twinkle. "Your sales for instance . . ."

"I know. I'm working on reversing the trend."

Wilbur sighed heavily. "Is everything all right? You'd come and see me if you had problems, wouldn't you?"

Matthew nodded. "Of course."

"Everything all right at home? Jennie and the boys?"

"They're away for a couple of weeks. They're staying with Jennie's parents on the farm."

Matthew failed to mention that they had gone away mainly to give Jennie breathing space, and time to think about the future of their marriage. Matthew realized that Wilbur was studying him carefully.

"There is a problem, isn't there?" he said. "Is there anything I can do to help?"

"Thanks, Wilbur. No, there's nothing wrong. Everything's fine."

Wilbur smiled. "Well, thank goodness for that. Two disasters in one day is about all I can manage. But I am concerned about your sales. You used to be so consistent, but now you're up and down and all over the place. I can't see any pattern to it, except that you're slowly slipping back. Let me know how we can help you get back where you were."

Somehow Matthew managed to finish the afternoon. He stopped at a bar on the way home, and had a few drinks by himself. He could not recall ever doing that before.

The house was dark when he got home. He had another beer, and then microwaved the dinner Jennie had prepared for him, the one labeled "Tuesday"—roast chicken with mushrooms and pasta. Normally, Matthew would have enjoyed the meal, but tonight it seemed lacking in taste. He sat in front of the television and watched the news. He absorbed none of it.

Instead he wondered why he hadn't told Wilbur about his problems. Every relationship went through ups and downs, he told himself. Why wasn't he able to confide in anyone? It might have helped to have told Wilbur about it, instead of pretending everything was fine. Wilbur would have sympathized, and that was the problem. He didn't want anyone's sympathy.

On an impulse he phoned his in-laws, but everyone was out and he was greeted by the answering machine.

"Sorry to miss you," he said after the beeping sound. "I hope the vacation's going well. I love you all. Good night."

It wasn't until he was getting ready for bed that he remembered that he hadn't looked in the mailbox. There were two bills and a white envelope that had his name and address written on it in perfect copper-plate handwriting.

Suddenly, he was thirty years younger, sitting in a high-school history class. Mr. Nevin was the only person he had ever known who wrote in such perfect handwriting. But he had to be dead. He was old thirty years ago. And why would he write to him now, after a gap of three decades?

He took the mail indoors and sat down again in front of the television. The sound of the program irritated him and he turned it off. He turned the envelope over and over several times. There was no return address and no stamp.

He opened the envelope slowly and carefully as if afraid to break the contents inside. The envelope contained one sheet of parchment paper. Copper-plate handwriting covered both sides. Matthew turned it over and looked at the signature. Franklin B. Nevin, his history teacher from all those many years ago.

Matthew's hands began to tremble. Mr. Nevin had sent him a letter. But why? After thirty years? Matthew stood up and walked around the room as he read the letter.

My dear Matthew,

How are you? Time flies when you get to my age. I can't remember what I did yesterday, but I vividly remember teaching you. Do you remember that day when you became absorbed in history, when that light bulb went off in your mind? I do. A teacher always remembers those moments, because they occur so seldom. Maybe five or six times in a forty-year career. I remember. I remember that day well. I could tell you the exact moment it happened, what we were discussing in class, who was paying attention, and who wasn't. I bet you remember what the topic was, even though it was so long ago. You always had an excellent memory.

And Matthew, do you remember those dreams of yours, all the great things you were going to do? I hope you've done them. Most people dream dreams and then dream some more. It's the people who seize their dreams and make them happen—they're the people who can change the world. Are you changing the world, Matthew?

Of course, we can change the world in many ways. Some people invent something that revolutionizes our whole way of life. Others compose music that stirs people's emotions. Some people teach and occasionally see a light bulb go off in a student's head. So even I, in my humble way, can make a small claim to changing the world. That is, if you and the others are doing what you should be doing. If you, and the handful of others I reached, are doing a fraction of what you told me you were going to do, the world is in good hands.

Matthew, do you remember the day I asked everyone in your class what they planned to do when they left school? Maybe you wondered why I wanted to know. I needed that information so that I could make my lessons relevant to everyone in the class. You might laugh, and say, "What's relevant about history?" but I'm sure I reached a few people by knowing what they were aiming for.

Some aimed high, others low. Do you remember Johnny Barber? He announced he was going to be president one day. He might have done it too, if he'd lived. Your class was a bright one. Your classmates told me they wanted to be accountants, lawyers, nuclear scientists, doctors, journalists. One wanted to be an entrepeneur. That's a common word today, but I heard it for the first time when he told me that in class. Howard's doing it. Do you remember what you wanted to do, Matthew? Are you doing it?

It's not too late, if you haven't started yet. It's never too late. Why, I got my Ph.D. in the end—at the age of seventy. My family called me an old fool, but I wanted to prove to myself that I could do it. I was passionate about it.

You've got to have a passion, Matthew. Tell me, what's yours?

One more thing. Be kind to yourself. We're all inclined to be harder on ourselves than we'd ever be on anyone else. Relax, and constantly bolster your self-esteem. Some people berate themselves for years over little things they did or didn't do. Let go of those. Forgive yourself, and move forward.

Well, that's all I want to say at the moment. I could ask if you're married or not, but I guess you are. I hope you have kids. You'd be a great dad.

I know I'm old and on the scrap heap. But I've lived a good life, Matthew. Being a teacher is not glamorous or exciting or well paid. But it was—and still is—my passion. I love seeing light bulbs going off.

Look after yourself Matthew,
Franklin B. Nevin

A tear trickled down Matthew's face as he read the letter. Once again he was in Mr. Nevin's classroom, listening as he explained the causes of the Civil War. And it was true—a lightbulb had gone off in his head that day. He'd become obsessed with history. In fact, he still was. All because of Mr. Nevin.

Occasionally, he had wondered why Mr. Nevin asked a class of fourteen-year-olds what they wanted to do in later life. How typical of Mr. Nevin to ask that question so that he could teach them better.

He had been terrified to tell everyone what his dream was. As Mr. Nevin had gone around the class and heard from people who wanted to become airline pilots and doctors, Matthew's throat had tightened more and more. When Mr. Nevin had asked him what he wanted to do, it had taken enormous effort to get the words out.

"Mr. Nevin, I want to be a salesman. I'm going to be a great salesman, just like my dad."

Mr. Nevin had nodded his head gently, gazed directly into Matthew's eyes and said, "You can do it,

Matthew. If that's what you really want to do, you can do it."

Why had he forgotten that dream? It had all been so simple when he was fourteen. Sure, he'd become a salesman, but he'd never been a *great* salesman. He'd never come close to what his dad had achieved.

An hour later, tossing and turning in bed, unable to sleep, Matthew wondered if it was really not too late. Was the passion still there? Did he still have a dream, or was he simply going through the motions of life?

As he finally drifted off to sleep, he silently thanked Mr. Nevin for contacting him.

"What's your passion?"

"Be kind to yourself."

Dear Matthew

Chapter Two

*M*ATTHEW'S EYES opened and he was instantly wide awake. He leaned over and looked at the bedside clock. Six in the morning. A whole hour before he usually woke up. He closed his eyes and tried to return to sleep, but too many thoughts were racing around inside his head.

He read Mr. Nevin's letter several times while eating breakfast. It was a shame that Mr. Nevin had not included his address, as he would have liked to let him know how much he had appreciated receiving it. He folded it and placed it in his shirt pocket before leaving for work.

Mr. Nevin was right, Matthew thought as he eased his way into the traffic. He had had a passion once. But that was a long time ago. What did he have now? It was hard to say.

He was at work by seven-thirty, and an hour later was up-to-date with the messages and correspondence on his desk. He was about to make himself some coffee when his phone rang. It was Mr. Bellowes, the president of Brazier Corporation.

"I arrived just after you," Mr. Bellowes boomed through the phone. "I like salespeople who are keen and eager. Come down and see me."

Matthew was used to Mr. Bellowes' gruff manner. He walked down the hallway and knocked on Mr. Bellowes' door. Following company policy, he did not wait for a response, but opened the door and walked in.

Mr. Bellowes was almost seventy, but still put in a sixty-hour week. He was short and portly, with a cheerful expression permanently etched on his face. A fringe of gray hair surrounded a gleaming bald spot. His eyes twinkled when he saw Matthew.

"Come in, boy," he said. "Have a seat."

At one time Matthew hated being called "boy," but now he was in his forties, he enjoyed it. Most of the time he didn't feel young.

"You're looking better this morning," Mr. Bellowes said. "Yesterday you seemed to have the whole world on your shoulders."

"It wasn't a good day," Matthew admitted. "But today's going to be much better."

Mr. Bellowes laughed. "Every morning when I get out of bed I tell myself that it's going to be a great day. And it usually is. Mind control." His smile slowly faded as he looked at Matthew. "Now I'm sure you've heard about the problems we're having with the Lochiel account."

Matthew nodded.

"Wilbur and Duncan are visiting them today. I'd like you to be there, too." He raised a hand when Matthew started to interrupt. "No, hear me out. Wilbur is a wonderful man, but he's gentle. Most of the time he gets the results we need, but in a quiet, roundabout way. Duncan's the opposite. He's loud and extroverted. Also, he's hurt and annoyed about what's happened. I need someone with no emotional involvement to accompany them. Someone with a good head."

Matthew gave him a lopsided grin. "Have you discussed this with Wilbur?"

Mr. Bellowes nodded. "Actually, Wilbur wanted me to come along, but I think we should save that possibility, in case we need it later. I'll call on their president, if need be, but I'd rather do that as a last resort. Will you go?"

"Sure, if you want me to." Matthew paused. "But why me?"

"You've got the maturity and the experience to handle this. Also, Wilbur thought it might do you good."

Roger Stacpole was a tall, thin man in his late thirties. His hair was blonde and receding, further lengthening his long, thin face. The party from Brazier arrived at the restaurant a few minutes early, but Roger was already seated when they arrived. He did not get up, and nodded unsmilingly as they slid into the booth.

For a few minutes, they talked about business in general, and how Brazier had supplied Lochiel with product for more than twenty years. The waitress arrived to take their orders, and when she left Wilbur said, "We've had a good record until now."

"You've been complacent, though," Roger said. "You've taken us for granted for years. When Duncan turned up ninety minutes late for our appointment, and barely apologized, I thought it was time we looked around."

Duncan tensed. He looked as if he was about to say something, but Matthew put a warning hand on his arm.

"Duncan tried to contact you," Wilbur said.

Roger shrugged. "So he said."

"I called a couple of times," Duncan said, his voice strained. "I should have left a message. I realize that now. But you were tied up both times, and I thought that as you were busy I'd just concentrate on getting to you as quickly as I could."

Roger shook his head. "That's not good enough. The least you could have done was leave a message."

"I agree," Wilbur said. "Duncan knows that now. The question is, what can we do to make this right again?"

Roger shook his head slowly, and pursed his lips. "It's too late for that. I waited an hour and a half for your man to arrive. When he didn't turn up, I called another company. They were delighted to get the order." He looked at Wilbur, a slight smirk on his face. "We're giving them a three-month trial."

Matthew tried to think. "But after twenty years of good service," he said. "Surely you could have given Duncan the benefit of the doubt. We've bent over backwards to help you people."

"And that's exactly what our new supplier has promised. I'm sure their sales reps will not keep me waiting, and I'm confident all their deliveries will be on time. Why don't you contact me again in a few months, and I'll let you know what their performance has been like."

Matthew and Wilbur pleaded and cajoled, but Roger was adamant. It was too late. He had committed Lochiel to the new supplier for a three-month trial, and he was not prepared to change that.

"If we were so bad that you needed to change suppliers," Wilbur said at the end of the meal, "Why did you never talk to me about the problems?"

Roger smiled. "Your service was never bad," he said. "But it was never spectacular, either."

"Did we supply on time?"

"Always."

"Did we hassle you about payment?"

Roger shook his head. "Not that I'm aware."

"Did Duncan keep you up-to-date on everything?"

Roger shrugged. "He was okay."

"Well, what did we do that was wrong?"

Roger briefly stretched and smiled at the waitress. He waited until Wilbur had paid the bill before answering.

"You did nothing wrong. I just think it's time for a change."

Matthew thought about the meeting as he drove to his next appointment. Although Roger had said they had done nothing wrong, that was not strictly correct. They had taken the Lochiel account for granted. Instead of treating them like a special account, Brazier had become lackadaisical. If Duncan had been calling on anyone else in the hope of picking up a $10,000 order, he would have been early, not late.

As he waited in the lobby for his client to arrive, Matthew reread Mr. Nevin's letter. By now, he virtually knew it by heart.

This time, he felt the light bulb switch on in his head. A wave of energy swept through his body. *Does that mean I still have a passion?* he wondered.

Matthew did not really expect another letter, but all the same, his anticipation mounted as he drove home. To his surprise and delight there was another white envelope in his mailbox, with the same copper-plate handwriting on it.

He carried it inside as if bearing the Holy Grail. He carefully opened it and pulled out the single sheet of paper, covered with beautiful handwriting. He felt his heart race, as he sat down in his comfortable chair and began to read.

My dear Matthew,

I've never sent two letters in less than two days to the same person in my whole life, not even when I was in love. However, something tells me that you need to hear from me.

Let me tell you something about myself. I'm an extremely rich man. Not in money terms, of course, though I've a little bit put aside. I'm rich because for most of my life I've done what I wanted to do.

I made up my mind to be a teacher when I was ten years old. Miss Frances was my teacher back then, and she inspired me. She set the light bulb off for me. My parents wanted me to go into business, and of course, they had my best interests at heart. I don't mind telling you there were times when it was hard to get by, bringing up four children on a teacher's salary. But it was what I had to do.

Do you understand that, Matthew? It's important. We all have something to do in this lifetime. It's our purpose, what we've been put here to do. Most people never find their purpose, their passion. That's sad, but it need not be the case. Look back over your life, Matthew, and think about the things you were good at, the things you loved to do. Are you doing them now? If not, why not? The things you enjoyed doing then often reveal your passion.

I had a friend years ago who loved sport, all sports. Unfortunately, his coordination was bad, and his eyesight wasn't so good. He was always the last person to be picked for games at school. That would have put me off, but it didn't worry him. He just loved playing sport. He loved talking about it, he even wrote about it. Well, when he left college he got a job at a radio station. Before you could blink an eye, he was commentating and reporting games on the air, and he ultimately became famous. You see, sport was his passion, and he made it his career. Not as a player—he could never have done that—but his enthusiasm and love shone through, and he became an outstanding reporter. Would he have achieved that, if it had just been a job?

Now let's get back to you. When you were fourteen, maybe fifteen, you told me of your passion. Selling. I remember you telling me that as if it was yesterday. You were scared to say it out loud in front of all the others, but you did. You said it proudly and with total conviction. Most of the kids who said they'd become lawyers and accountants didn't say it from the heart, the way you did. If they ever made the grade and became accountants or whatever, do you think they love their work? Are they passionate about it? Or is it just a meal ticket?

I believed you when you told me of your passion. I believed maybe two or three others in the room that day. Why? Because they had passion also.

Passion isn't enough on its own, of course. You need determination. You need persistence. You need something to aim for, a goal. That's why we need dreams, Matthew. You dreamed of being a great salesman. You saw yourself doing it. You could sense it, feel it, even taste it. I can empathize with that. That's how I felt about teaching.

Do you remember Mr. Stokes, the janitor? Probably not. He was the invisible person who kept the school clean and presentable. Most people looking at him would consider him a failure. Not me. Mr. Stokes and I became good friends. I could see the care and attention he put into his job. He put more into his job than anyone else at the school. He loved his job,

Matthew, and he cried the day they forced him to retire. He loved what he did. Do you love what you do?

Oh, we all have bad days. I've had my share. Trying to teach people who didn't want to learn. Kids who were aggressive and abusive. I had a kid bring a gun into class once. You don't forget those things. But I don't dwell on that. I think about the handful of people I influenced positively. That's why I'm writing this to you.

You see, most of the time I choose my thoughts. I have bad thoughts and good thoughts. Negative and positive. We all do. I try to focus on the positive ones. It's not easy sometimes. There were times when I wanted to give up, and just walk away. Leave everything behind. I'm sure you've felt that way, too. We all do. But you have strength of character. You didn't give up. You kept on going. That's persistence.

Now, we're coming to the point of this letter. I always rambled, didn't I? It's a sign of a good teacher, I think. If you have a teacher like that, you can learn about all sorts of things. You can learn about life.

Now the point of this letter. Are you following your dream, Matthew? Do you have something you want to do that scares you? Terrifies you? I hope so, Matthew. You need something big and worthwhile ahead of you, something to seize and run with. It doesn't matter if you never reach it, just as long as you aim high and work steadily towards your goal. Enjoy the journey, Matthew. The journey is more important than reaching the goal. If you aim high and work towards something you consider worthwhile, you'll have no regrets when you're lying on your death bed. You'll have given life your best shot.

I hope you don't mind these letters, Matthew. I feel that you need some encouragement right now. I hope my musings help clarify things in your mind. And I'm not being totally altruistic. Writing my thoughts down like this helps me, too.

I'll be in touch again soon.

Franklin B. Nevin

It was hunger that brought Matthew back to the present. He looked at his watch. Nine-thirty. He had sat at the table for three hours. It was funny, but he could swear that Mr. Nevin had been sitting there with him.

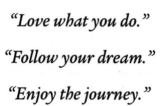

"Love what you do."

"Follow your dream."

"Enjoy the journey."

Dear Matthew

Chapter Three

Again Matthew awoke at six in the morning, and was in the office by seven-thirty. He heard Mr. Bellowes arrive shortly before eight and followed him into his office.

"We'll have to send your wife away more often," Mr. Bellowes laughed. "You've beaten me to work two days in a row!"

Matthew joined in the laughter. For a moment he contemplated telling Mr. Bellowes about the letters, but decided to keep silent, at least for the present. "With Jennie away, it's a good chance to get on top of things."

Mr. Bellowes nodded. "You're a lucky man, having a loving wife and kids." He raised a forefinger sternly. "Take care of them. They're your greatest possession." Matthew remembered that Mr. Bellowes had been widowed for many years. He had never heard him mention any children. Mr. Bellowes leaned forward in his chair. "Wilbur told me about your lunch. It seems the Lochiel account has gone elsewhere, at least for a few months."

"Duncan'll keep a close eye on the situation."

Mr. Bellowes raised an eyebrow, and for a moment his smile vanished. "If the account's been lost, you reps will have to make up the difference somehow. You'll all have to increase sales. Better yet, find another big account." He sighed heavily, "We've had situations like this before, of course," he continued. "We've always survived. It's up to you guys to keep the figures up. So far you've had an easy run here, Matthew. Now it's time you earned your pay."

Wilbur had a sales meeting in his office at nine. The sales team was subdued, and there were none of the usual jokes and jibes before Wilbur began.

"Sales will be well down for the next few months unless we do something quickly." Wilbur cleared his throat and interlaced his fingers. He sounded nervous, but was more forceful when he spoke again.

"We need as many of the new season's orders as possible, but we also need to find ourselves another big account. How can we achieve this?"

Matthew was surprised to find himself suggesting ideas.

"If you like, I could also help out in the northeast until you find a replacement for Sam."

Wilbur laughed. "Thanks for the offer, Matthew, but I don't think so. Jennie would make my life miserable! Concentrate on your own territory and see if you can find us another good account."

Matthew was disappointed that Wilbur was opposed to him spending time on the road, but was happy that some of his other ideas had been accepted. Driving between calls he realized that he may have offered his services more to get out of town and away from his personal problems than from any real desire to help. Obviously, Wilbur was more astute that he had thought.

The day was busy and he arrived home exhausted. He ran out to get the mail, but there was no letter from Mr. Nevin.

The following morning, Wilbur interviewed two people for Sam's position. Both of them were given a tour of the sales department. The first was a thirty-five-year-old man who had had a great deal of selling experience. Unfortunately, though, he had worked for more than twenty companies in a fifteen-year period.

The second one's résumé did not look promising, except for his name: Bernie Nevin.

He was tall, confident, and gazed directly into Matthew's eyes as they shook hands. He had a kindly, rugged face, and wore a pleasant smile. He looked a few years older than the twenty-seven years written on his job application.

"I used to know someone called 'Nevin,'" Matthew said. "Many years ago, he taught me at school. His name was Franklin. Franklin B. Nevin." The precise signature at the bottom of the two letters sprang into his mind. "Are you related to him?"

Bernie nodded. "Oddly enough, I am. He was my great uncle. My grandfather's brother, actually." He waved a hand deprecatingly. "We're not a close family. I haven't seen him for, let's see, at least fifteen years, maybe more. Is he still alive?"

Matthew nodded. "He certainly is. I've received a couple of letters from him. He seems to be busy and active."

Bernie smiled. "I'm pleased to hear it. As I said, we're not a close family."

Matthew sighed. "I doubt if any of us are as good as we should be in that area."

Matthew met a client for a drink after work. The meeting progressed on to dinner, and he arrived home at ten-thirty. He was almost asleep when he remembered that he hadn't checked the mail. There was only one letter in the mailbox. Matthew recognized Mr. Nevin's beautiful handwriting before the envelope was in his hand. He ran indoors and carefully opened the envelope.

Dear Matthew,

Times are tough. When you think about it, times are always tough. But there are opportunities everywhere, no matter how tough the times. And when times are tough, you have a chance to show your mettle. You have the right stuff, Matthew. You can seize an opportunity and make it happen. Times are tough for you right now. But tough times don't last. Tough people do.

Let me tell you what I used to do in tough times. I'd make three lists. One of the things I wanted to achieve. The second list would be the worst possible scenario. For instance, I might have wanted everyone in my class to pass a certain test. Not easy, but possible. What happened if not everyone passed?

Well, nothing really, except that *I'd* feel disappointed, as if I'd failed, rather than the students. So on one list I'd write my goal for the class. On the other list I'd write down the outcome if I did not succeed, how disappointed I'd feel. The third list was the opposite. On that one I'd write down the outcome if I succeeded. With this scenario, it would be feelings of pride and satisfaction. In the business world it's a little different. Success could mean a pay raise, a bigger commission. Failure could mean loss of a job.

So why do I do it? I've already told you not to dwell on the negative. Yet here I am writing down the worst possible outcomes in a list. Let me explain. It seems to me that we always make things worse than they are. You might think that when something fails to work it is absolutely devastating, but when you come to write down the worst possible outcome, it might be minor. So small, in fact, that you wonder why you worried about it. The positive list acts as motivation. We all want to feel good, to be rewarded, noticed. Usually, you'll find, that the best scenario offers more pluses than the other list does minuses. It helps you put things in perspective, and Matthew, you haven't being putting things in perspective.

Whenever you're having problems at work, write down three lists: what you want to achieve, the worst possible outcome, and the best outcome. It's like goal-setting, but with rewards and penalties added.

Don't just do this for work, Matthew. Do it for other areas of your life as well. You'll be amazed at the clarity of vision it will give you.

You'll receive another letter from me tomorrow. It's important that you do this exercise before reading the next letter.

Kind regards,
Franklin B. Nevin

Matthew read the letter several times. He put on his bathrobe, collected pen and paper, and sat down at the dining-room table.

He wrote "What I want" on the first sheet of the pad, and stared at the words for five minutes. Finally he wrote "Get my sales back to what they were." It didn't seem enough. He crossed it out and wrote "Increase my sales by 10 percent." It took ten minutes to come up with anything else. After half an hour he had a small list:

> Increase my sales by 10 percent
> Find a new account that is better than Lochiel

> Become best salesperson in the corporation
> Motivate and inspire myself and others
> Spend quality time with family
> Tell Jennie how much I love her

He read the list aloud, and then added one final line:

> Become a great salesman

He smiled and went out to the kitchen to make a cup of tea. When he returned, he began on the worst possible outcomes list.

Theoretically, he could lose his job if he failed to increase his sales. He contemplated this thought for a while. It was an unlikely prospect, but even if it did happen, it wasn't the end of the world. He'd quickly find other work.

If he could not find an account that was better than the Lochiel one, there would be no immediate penalty, except to his pride. The same thing applied if he failed to become the best salesperson in the corporation.

Motivating and inspiring himself and others was extremely important, and was something he was usually good at. His sales were declining only because he was finding it hard to remain motivated at present. Unless he changed his attitude, his sales would continue their downward trend, and eventually he would lose his job.

If he failed to spend quality time with his family, or tell them all how much he loved them, he would ultimately lose them.

If he failed to become a great salesperson, he was the only person who would ever know. However, what would he feel like ten or twenty years from now if he failed to achieve his childhood dream?

Finally, he could see why Mr. Nevin had suggested he prepare this list.

The Positive Outcome list was much easier to write. In fact, it all sounded too good to be true. Work would become a joy if he increased his sales by 10 percent. A new account that was better than the Lochiel one would ensure a good Christmas bonus, plus many other benefits. Becoming the best salesperson in the corporation would provide much greater remuneration, opportunities for promotion, and possibly job offers from other corporations. Motivating and inspiring himself and others would provide increased sales. This, coupled with regaining the Lochiel account and finding an even bigger new account, would make Brazier Corporation the biggest of its kind in the industry.

The two home and family outcomes were easy to imagine, and Matthew smiled as he wrote down how wonderful life would be if he achieved those goals.

He paused at the final one. "Become a great salesman."

"Just like my dad," he said aloud.

What would life be like if he achieved that goal? He'd be fulfilling a lifelong dream, but was it realistic? Could he ever do it now?

After a long pause, he wrote just one word:

Happiness.

"Keep things in perspective."

"Focus on the positive."

Dear Matthew

Chapter Four

THE FOLLOWING few days were difficult. The usual Friday sales meeting was a disaster. Sam Mulligan failed to turn up, no doubt because he was leaving. Wilbur was obviously annoyed, although he tried to conceal it. He had wanted to ask Sam questions about his territory and key customers. Duncan was uncooperative, probably because he felt embarrassed and humiliated at losing the Lochiel account. Mr. Bellowes appeared briefly. He told everyone that he had full confidence that they would turn the sales around, and then left.

After that, it was hard to inspire the team. Wilbur kept the meeting short and arranged to have a few words with everyone privately. The reps appeared to enjoy the one-on-one attention, and Wilbur said he would make it a regular part of his work.

Wilbur interviewed four more applicants for Sam's position, none of whom were suitable. Avril phoned Bernie Nevin and arranged for him to come in for a second interview. She contacted Bernie's previous employer and found that he had been excellent at his job, but had wanted a change. They were sorry to see him go.

Bernie was just as casual this time. He seemed totally unconcerned about getting the job.

"I enjoyed it," he told Wilbur, when asked about his previous work. "But it was only a means to an end. I did phone sales, as part of my work, but I really wanted to be out in the field. There were no openings where I was, so I quit."

"Most people find another position before leaving the first one."

Bernie laughed. "Not me! You see, I was due for a vacation, so it doesn't worry me if it takes a while to get a new job. This way I can spend all my time looking for the right one."

"Does this sound like the right one?"

Bernie grinned and nodded vigorously. "This is the position I've been looking for. I'll do a good job for you."

Wilbur had lingering doubts but offered him a three-month trial. Bernie agreed to start on Monday.

Matthew read Mr. Nevin's letters several times every day. He spent hours going over the three lists he had made. On Friday morning, he decided to pay a surprise visit to his in-laws, to see Jennie and the boys.

After work, he went home to pack a few things, and found another letter from Mr. Nevin in the mailbox.

Dear Matthew,
I hope you've been thinking about your life and where it is going. Today we're going to talk about the inner you. Your external life reflects the inner you. I'm sure you know the saying "As a man thinketh in his heart, so is he." We're going to talk about your heart and soul. Where do you think passion comes from, Matthew? From your heart and soul. This sounds wishy-washy to some people, but it is vital to understand this if you are going to achieve everything you desire.

Have you made three lists yet? Here's an exercise for you to do with them. Take the list of things you want to achieve, and read the first item out loud. Wait a few moments and see if you feel any reaction in your body. You might feel something in your heart, your lower back, across your shoulders, your stomach, anywhere. See what that feeling tells you. Then, let it go, and do the same thing with all the other items on your list.

Which items made you feel good? You might have felt a glow in your heart as you read them, or maybe your back straightened and you felt ready to overcome everything that stands in the path to your success.

Which items made you feel tense? Or nervous, or scared, or afraid? Those items are stress producing. Look at them carefully, and see if you really want to achieve them. Of course, you can still achieve them if you are determined enough, but you will have to change your attitude to them first. Otherwise, you'll find they'll drain you of enthusiasm and motivation.

We all do the things that we really want to do. That's because they're easy. They're fun. We have the motivation, the energy, the enthusiasm. But we all have other tasks that need to be done. Are you like me, Matthew? Do you leave those things until the last moment? That's because they're hard work, and we don't really want to do them anyway.

I'm sure there are items like this on your list. Select one of them, and go for a long walk by yourself. Think about this goal, and why you want to achieve it. Think of the rewards—you've already written them down on another list. Think about what happens if you don't achieve it. See if you can change your attitude about this goal or project. Then, when you get back home, sit down and think about the goal again, and see how it feels in your body this time. If it feels right, do it. Make it happen. If it still feels stressful or uncomfortable, think about it some more. Ponder it while you're driving in the car, or sitting down quietly somewhere. Meditate on it, if you wish. Remember, be prepared for problems if you try to do it without receiving comfortable feelings in your body first.

You've heard of the mind-body connection. They're more closely connected than you'd imagine. Many years ago I had to see my bank manager about my overdraft. He wanted it reduced. We came to an agreement on how I could do it, and I left him feeling positive and confident. However, a couple of hours later, I experienced chronic lower back pain. Pain in the lower back is often related to money, Matthew. Although I knew I could do everything my bank manager wished, my body still reacted. You must listen to your body all the time.

And while you're doing that, listen to your soul. Listen to your heart. Listen to your intuition. You'll become in tune with your inner power. You'll realize that your potential is limitless. That means totally without limits.

Focus on love. The love you have for others, naturally. But tell me, do you love your work? Do you love what you do with a passion? If you became financially independent today, would you keep on doing what you're doing now? If you died tomorrow, would you be happy with what you have achieved in this lifetime?

You probably think I'm getting morbid in my old age. I'm not. Years ago I did a survey of the other teachers at our school. I can't remember if it was while you were there, or not. It doesn't matter. Most of them had lost interest in teaching. The joy, the enthusiasm, the love had disappeared. Obviously, it was time for them to move in other directions where they'd feel more fulfilled, but not one of them did. Fear held them back. That meant they led crippled half-lives. They suffered, and their students suffered, too.

Don't lead a half-life, Matthew. I'm trying to help you find your passion. When you find your passion you'll never work again. Of course, you'll probably work extremely hard, but it won't seem like work. And then, if you win millions of dollars, you'll carry on with whatever it is you are doing. Because it is your passion, your purpose, your reason for being here.

Get busy with that exercise, Matthew.

Best wishes,

Franklin B.

Jennie's parents lived on a small farm at the end of a dusty road that wound through a long valley. It was ten-thirty when Matthew arrived. He took a deep breath and rolled his shoulders to ease the tension after the four-hour drive.

His heart lit up as soon as he opened the car door and heard the happy sounds of his children playing inside. He was thrilled that they were still awake. Shep, his in-laws' collie, began barking, and the outside light was turned on.

"It's dad!" he heard Jason call out.

Before he had time to grab his bag from the backseat, he was enveloped in a hug from Jason and Eric, both excited to see him, and each asking questions at the same time. Jennie ran out, too, and the whole family hugged each other.

"What a great surprise," Jennie said, as they made their way indoors. "I called you just an hour ago and got the machine. I thought you were out with some work friends."

Matthew looked around the large farmhouse kitchen. "I'd much rather be here." He grinned at Jennie and the boys. "Much rather."

Jennie's parents came in, and Ellen insisted on making supper for everyone. Matthew felt happier than he had been for months as he sat at the big wooden table and watched his sons eat most of the hot scones. He put his arm around Jennie and smiled.

"This is fantastic," he said. "Out in the country with the people I love. It's hard to believe that just a few hours ago I was in the city."

"We'll let you sleep in tomorrow," Jack, his father-in-law, said. "Then you can help me with the fencing. Give you a chance to breathe some good, fresh country air."

Matthew felt as if he had already had a vacation by the time he and Jennie went to bed in a huge four-poster bed in the guest bedroom. He held her close and kissed her tenderly.

"There's something I want to tell you," he said. He smelled the clean freshness of her hair.

"Mmmm," Jennie replied.

"I want you to know how much I love you and the boys. The three of you mean everything to me. I couldn't live without you."

Jennie pulled away and looked closely at him.

"What's brought this on?" she said. "Why are you saying this now?"

"It's just, well, I've missed you all week, and I guess it's given me time to think. It's not home without you. I can hardly wait for you all to be back again." He leaned forward and gently stroked her cheek.

"Maybe we should go away more often." She put her arms around him and held him tightly. "I love you, too, you know," she continued.

"But, but you went away to think about things, including us."

"That's because you haven't been your usual self. You've been distracted lately, Matthew. There's been tension in the house. Even the boys noticed it. We needed a break, but it will be good to be home again next week." She kissed him on the nose. "I'm glad you're here."

When Matthew awoke the following morning the house was quiet. He looked at his watch: nine-fifty. It had been years since he had slept that late.

He showered, dressed, and went downstairs. Breakfast had been laid out for him. There was also a note from Jennie explaining that they had gone to the local store.

They returned home while he was rinsing the dishes. The boys came running in with a soccer ball that Ellen had bought for them.

"Come on, Dad," Jason said. "Let's have kicks on the front lawn."

Matthew laughed and happily joined the boys in a two against one game of soccer. When Ellen called them in for lunch he couldn't believe how quickly the time had flown.

"Can we do this again after lunch?" Eric asked.

Matthew patted him on the head. "Sure we can."

Jack came in and jokingly chastised Matthew for not waking up in time to help him. After lunch, Jack watched them play for a while, and then suggested they visit a swimming hole in the river.

In bed that night, Matthew said, "You know, my body's talking to me." He smiled at the strange look in Jennie's face. "My shoulders have been so tight and tense, but they've completely let go. I'm exhausted, but I feel better than I've felt in years."

"We should come out to the farm more often."

Matthew nodded. "We should. You and I are getting time to talk. I've played with the boys. I've had a marvelous day."

Jennie snuggled up to him. "And it's not over yet."

"Listen to your body."

"Your potential is limitless."

Dear Matthew

Chapter Five

MATTHEW GOT back home shortly after ten on Sunday night. He felt tired, but decided to do the exercise Mr. Nevin had suggested about seeing what his goals felt like in his body.

He began by reading Mr. Nevin's letters again. It was an uncanny feeling. It seemed as if Mr. Nevin was in the room with him. He smiled at his foolishness, and said the first goal aloud.

"Increase my sales by 10 percent."

He paused to see what his body had to say. For a while it seemed as if nothing was going to happen, but then he felt a gradual tightening across his shoulders. He rolled his shoulders a few times and read out the second goal.

"Find a new account that is better than the Lochiel one."

He paused expectantly. There was nothing discernible in his body, but a feeling of quiet pleasure passed through him. On an impulse, he asked a question.

"Was Bernie Nevin a good choice?"

Immediately, he felt the tension lift from his shoulders. Why had he never noticed these things before?

"Become best salesperson in the corporation."

His stomach responded with a sense of nervousness.

"Can I do it?" The nervousness subtly changed to a feeling of excitement.

"Will I do it?" The flow of adrenaline throughout his body was unmistakable.

"Motivate and inspire myself and others."

He felt no response from his body.

"Motivate and inspire myself and others," he repeated. Again there was no response at all. Suddenly, the adrenaline flowed, and Matthew laughed with delight.

"Spend quality time with my family."

He was unprepared for the response his body gave him. He felt a sudden warmth and surge of power in his heart. It felt as if he was expanding inside his chest.

"Tell Jennie how much I love her." He'd already done that. The warm glow remained in his chest, but he felt a tightening in his throat. The pressure suddenly let go and he felt a warmth in his neck that quickly spread to every part of his body.

"Thank you, Mr. Nevin," he said out loud. "You've helped me more than you could possibly imagine."

Matthew hummed tunelessly as he walked into the sales office the following morning. Avril looked at him curiously, but made no comment.

Bernie Nevin arrived a few minutes later, looking as relaxed as ever.

"Good morning," he said cheerfully. "Where shall I start?"

Wilbur had Avril take him around the building to introduce him to everyone. Afterward, they returned to the sales office and found Sam Mulligan.

Sam opened up his database and explained the needs of each account to Bernie. Wilbur stood behind Sam, and made occasional comments. Bernie busily made notes, and asked questions. Matthew, working at his desk, was pleased to see that most of the questions were phrased towards gaining more business.

"We need to find someone to replace Lochiel," Wilbur said when Sam finished. "Some of those look promising, but none of them have the potential to replace Lochiel. Is there anyone else in your area we should contact?"

Sam nodded. "Definitely. That was my customer list. I have another file of prospects." A few taps on the keyboard and the file came into view. "These are all people I've tried to get business from, without success. This column here shows how many times I've contacted them."

There were twenty-two names in the file. Bernie asked for a printout of both lists.

A small student's desk had been placed next to Sam, and Bernie spent an hour seated here going over the printouts. He asked Avril for regional directories, and made several more lists. After lunch, he asked for Internet access.

"There must be many more prospects," he said. "I'll download as many of them as I can, and then tomorrow I'll start making calls."

Wilbur was delighted with his keenness, but suggested that he spend a week or so in the office to learn about the company's products.

Bernie shook his head. "I'll take material home to read up on," he said. "But it looks as if you need a major new client right away. I want to get started on that."

Matthew wondered how long his enthusiasm would last.

Wilbur seemed to have no misgivings. He asked Matthew if he could help Bernie get started.

"Just for a day or two." Matthew detected a pleading look in his eyes. "And only while your family are away."

"All right," Matthew said. "Tell you what, Bernie. Tomorrow you and I'll make some calls. You can do the work, and I'll provide the product knowledge, if needed." He looked at his watch. "There's still time to make some appointments."

Dear Matthew,
I'm thrilled that you're acting on my suggestions. I hope it's making a difference. You know all about the importance of a good attitude. Without it, you're doomed to failure. With a good attitude, a worthwhile goal, and plenty of drive and persistence, there's no limit to how far you can go. You'll also set a good example to your children. Listen to your heart every day,

and you won't go wrong. Listen to that quiet little voice inside. It knows everything, and will tell you what you need to know. It's true, Matthew. Your soul knows everything. Be ruled by your soul, Matthew. Too many people are ruled by their egos. I'm sure you've met many of them.

People who are ruled by their egos have low self-esteem. Sure, they may look big and important and powerful, but they're small inside. They need the approval of others. Without it, they crumble and fail.

What is your source of personal power, Matthew? Is it money? Power? Possessions? We all have egos, and they have needs that can hold you back. Forget your ego, Matthew, and look inward. Your soul knows everything, and if you make it your source of personal power, you will achieve more in a month than many people achieve in a lifetime.

Do things because you love to do them, Matthew. Not because they make you money or bolster your ego. Remember what I said: *Find your passion and you'll never need to work again.*

Let's talk about your mind, Matthew. You have a good mind. I remember it well. Where is your mind, Matthew? Is it in your head? Somewhere in your brain? Could it be in your big toe? Of course, there's no answer to this, as no one knows where your mind is. Maybe it's not in your body at all. And is it *your* mind, your mind exclusively, or is it part of something much larger, a universal mind, perhaps? Is it, perhaps, your soul?

Your soul is immortal. It existed before you were born, and it will continue to exist long after the physical body you currently inhabit has died. What does it feel like to be immortal, Matthew?

We have lessons to learn here, Matthew. Important lessons. And I believe that if they are not learned in this lifetime, you come back again and again until they are learned.

What do you need to learn? All sorts of things. But finding your passion, and running with it, taking it further than you ever believed possible, means that in this lifetime you'll make great progress.

Ask your body if you are a great salesman, and listen to what it says.

I'll be in touch very soon.

Franklin

How did he know? Matthew wondered. He had asked his body about everything on the list, except becoming a great salesman.

He took several deep breaths, closed his eyes, and spoke aloud: "Could I become a great salesman?"

It took several seconds for his body to respond. It began with a surge of power in his solar plexus that spread through his chest and up into his head. The feeling lasted for half a minute, until Matthew let it go.

"Really?" he said aloud, looking around the room as if seeing it for the first time. "Yes, I can. I'm going to become a great salesman!"

The following morning he picked up Bernie at seven-thirty for the two-hour drive up to Sam's territory. Despite heavy traffic, they arrived at the first appointment right on time. As the day progressed, Matthew became increasingly impressed with Bernie's natural ease and skill at dealing with people. He had obviously studied the sales material, too, and was able to make suggestions for additional purchases to everyone they called on.

They finished the final appointment at four-thirty and Matthew decided to test his new salesman.

"Why don't we do a cold call before heading back?" he asked.

Bernie grinned. "That's a great idea, boss. Who shall we call on?"

They selected a name at random from the list of prospects that Bernie had compiled the previous day. Unfortunately, the premises were closed when they arrived, but Bernie promised to call on them in the following few days.

"Hey, Matthew, why don't I stay up here for a day or two and call on everyone? That is, if you think I'm ready."

Matthew headed home on his own. It was too early to tell, but it looked as if Bernie was going to make an excellent representative. Mind you, it was one thing to do all the calls when someone else was present. How hard would he work when he was on his own? Time would tell.

Matthew smiled as he thought about his first sales job. Mr. Kelly, the sales manager, had set him loose, exactly as he had just done with Bernie. "You sink or swim," Mr. Kelly had told him. "It's up to you."

And he had swum. It had taken a while, but Matthew was motivated and determined. He wanted to be a great salesman, just like his father.

In the end, it wasn't anything his father had taught him that ensured success. It was a simple line, almost tossed away, that Mr. Kelly had said one day.

"You know, when I was on the road, at the end of each day when I'd finished my work, I'd make one more call. One extra call every day gave me 250 more prospects a year. That's how I became sales manager."

It was how Matthew had made his mark as well.

The traffic had slowed down because of roadwork, and Matthew glanced across the freeway at a large office building. There were lights on in the ground floor, and he could just make out a man working at a desk.

If this had been my territory, I'd have called on him, he thought. My last call for the day.

Although he thought he had discarded the idea as soon as it occurred, he found himself getting off the freeway at the first exit and doubling back to the office building. The main entrance was locked, and he almost returned to his car. His father's determination came into his mind. Dad would not have been defeated by this. Emboldened, Matthew knocked on the plate glass doors.

There was no response, so Matthew walked around the building to the office he had seen from the freeway. A smartly dressed man was sitting behind his desk, studying some papers. He jumped when Matthew tapped on the window.

Matthew held up his business card. Although the man was obviously not able to read it from where he sat, he indicated the main entrance, and Matthew went back to wait for him.

An hour later, he again headed home, a contented smile on his face. Yes, Mr. Kelly would have been proud of him. So would his father. He hadn't received an order, but the man had been so impressed with Matthew's approach that he'd offered him a job. His name was Tom Gozinski, and he was heading a startup company in the computer industry. It was a good contact, and he'd have to remember to ask Bernie to follow up on it.

Although there was no new letter from Mr. Nevin in the mailbox, and his family was still away, Matthew felt happy as he lay in bed waiting for sleep.

"I am a great salesman," he said to himself. The feeling began again in his solar plexus and moved upwards.

"I love Jennie and the boys." The glow in his heart was almost too much to bear.

"I am a lucky man." A feeling of peace and happiness spread over him, and he drifted into sleep.

"Find your source of personal power."

"What do you need to learn?"

Dear Matthew

Chapter Six

*M*ATTHEW ARRIVED at work shortly after seven. He was surprised to find that Wilbur had arrived before him. The phone was ringing in his office when he walked in.

"I want to see you," Wilbur said.

This was unlike Wilbur, and Matthew hurried through to his office to see what the problem was. Wilbur's eyes were bloodshot and he looked exhausted. Instead of greeting him, Wilbur waved a sheaf of computer printouts in the air.

"Have you seen these?" he asked. "The sales are pathetic."

"I wasn't in the office yesterday. I spent the day with Bernie."

Wilbur said nothing. Instead, he handed Matthew the computer printouts and stared out the window while Matthew went through them.

"Surely these are seasonal fluctuations," Matthew said, after going through the list. "I can see a few areas that need to be looked at, and I'll get on to them right away. But, I doubt that you'd have commented on these figures if the Lochiel order had been included."

Wilbur turned around, frustration written all over his face.

"But we can't include the Lochiel figures, because we don't have them. We didn't get the order." He waved his hands in the air. "What we need is more orders. Lots of them. Please, Matthew. We need orders."

Matthew had never seen Wilbur like this before. The situation was obviously more serious than the sales staff realized. On the spur of the moment, Matthew told him about the letters he had been receiving, and offered to let him read them. Matthew returned to his office thoughtfully.

The day proved to be a hectic one. Bernie phoned several times. He was finding work much harder on his own. Matthew agreed to spend two days with him next week. Duncan had lost all his confidence after the Lochiel fiasco, and Wilbur virtually had to order him out of the office to make his calls.

Matthew drove home through the rush-hour traffic, trying not to think of all the things that had to be done. While waiting for a green light, he thought about leaving Brazier and finding a less stressful job, but quickly discarded the idea. His father had never flinched from a challenge. Only cowards jump when things get tough, he told himself. Even Wilbur had looked and sounded more positive after reading the letters. If they could find some way to motivate and inspire everyone, Brazier's would move ahead again. The big problem was everyone's mental attitude.

Matthew said his affirmations out loud as he drove the last couple of miles home. A familiar-looking envelope was waiting for him.

He forced himself to change into casual clothes. He poured himself a beer, and then opened Mr. Nevin's letter.

Dear Matthew,
There's an old saying, "When the going gets tough, the tough get going." I hope that's what you're doing, as I sense that you're not having

a smooth ride at present. Keep focused on the positive, and ignore the negative. You'll always find negative people who want to pull you down. You'll encounter every sort of person as you go through life. People can be happy, sad, lonely, stressed, angry, confused, even crazy. Just remember, Matthew, that every person you meet has a beautiful soul, even if all you see is tension or rage. You have to look beyond the person's faults, and see the beauty within. If you can do that, you'll be a rich man.

Imagine looking at someone, observing his faults, but still seeing the beauty within. When you can do that, you'll be able to inspire others with your example. You'll be able to help people rise above their limitations and become successful and fulfilled. That's what I tried to do with my students. I saw them as small plants that needed to be nurtured and loved, so that one day, they would become everything they could be. If just one of those plants turned into a beautiful flower, I would be well rewarded.

Nurture others, Matthew. Don't put others down. If you can look through their faults and see the beautiful soul inside, you'll react differently. I promise you that the rewards of this approach are beyond measure.

You're probably wondering why I'm going on about souls all the time, Matthew. I'm not trying to force my beliefs onto you. I hope you have a spiritual side to your life. We all need to believe in something, and a personal faith is an enormous help, not just when times are difficult, but all the time. If you have no faith, Matthew, please read, study, meditate, and search until you find something that is right for you. Find something to believe in. It will give purpose to your life. And while I'm talking about faith, you must have faith in yourself.

Think about these things, Matthew. You may think that they have nothing to do with being a "great salesman," but in fact, they have everything to do with your success in sales, or any other endeavor. These are not my secrets, Matthew. They are old, and if you study the life of any great person you will find that they used these ideas to achieve their goals.

I predict that from now on, no matter what happens in your life, you will see much more beauty around you, and in the soul of everyone you meet.

Times might be tough right now, but keep a good, positive attitude. Eliminate fear, doubt, and worry, and replace them with determination, enthusiasm, and persistence.

You have a beautiful soul, Matthew.

Franklin

P.S. You have my blessing to share these letters with others, if you feel they will benefit from them.

Matthew read the letter several times during the evening. He read it one last time before turning out the light. It was hard to see what Mr. Nevin was getting at. He had always gotten along well with others. He never deliberately put anyone down. Of course, there were times when he'd said things he later regretted, but he was not alone in doing that.

The next morning brought several answers. He arrived at work early, but Mr. Bellowes, Wilbur, and Avril were all there before him.

"I had a lot to catch up on," Avril explained when he asked why she had come in so early.

"I really appreciate everything you do," Matthew told her. "I know I don't thank you often enough, but I think you're wonderful. The way you keep on top of things makes us all look good, even though you're the one who's done all the work. Thank you very much."

He smiled at the surprised look on her face, and went through to the sales office. He received several other surprised looks from different people as the day progressed, and he finally realized what he was doing. He was noticing and appreciating people more than ever before. Was he perhaps starting to see their souls?

He returned to the office late in the afternoon. Duncan was slumped behind his desk, looking tired and glum. When Matthew tried to cheer him up, he squirmed in his chair.

"I'm not usually depressed like this," he said. "And you've been extremely supportive. But it's my fault we lost the Lochiel account. If I'd been there on time, or if I'd managed to get through to Roger Stacpole, we'd still have that order."

Matthew saw the tension and anxiety around Duncan's eyes. "That's water under the bridge now," he said. "Naturally, it would be great to have the account back, but we can't live in the past. We have to face facts, and accept that that account has gone, at least in the short term. I know how hard you've been trying to get it back."

"I was just too complacent. Roger always seemed easygoing. I didn't expect him to react like this."

"People are complicated. They don't always do what we expect, or what we want them to do. Anyway, Brazier existed well before we had the Lochiel account. We'll survive, with or without their orders." Matthew surprised himself with the enthusiasm in his voice. "It might be a bit harder in the short term, but you can help in that regard. What we need is the old Duncan back. The Duncan who enjoyed a challenge, who took calculated risks, who wrote up lots of orders. We need a new, improved Duncan, one who has learned a few lessons, and is determined to succeed. Does that sound like you?"

Matthew spoke quietly, but as he spoke Duncan sat up straight in his chair and life returned to his eyes.

"Do you think I can do it?"

Matthew grinned. "Would I have said that if I didn't think you could? We all make mistakes, Duncan. I should know. I've made tons of them. It doesn't matter as long as we learn from them, and move ahead. I know you can do it."

There was another letter from Mr. Nevin in the mailbox. Matthew felt his spirits rise as he carried it inside.

My dear Matthew,
I hope I didn't alarm you with the metaphysical nature of my last letter. In many ways, it's the most important letter I've written to you. Once you start seeing people's souls, you'll change enormously. You'll be more understanding, less judgmental. More forgiving,

more at peace inside yourself. People will respond to you in quite a different way. They will start to see your beautiful soul. Read my last letter again, Matthew. Read it again and again until it makes perfect sense to you. The message is simple, but it can change your life.

Now, here's another tip that can change your life. You're a busy man, Matthew. Too busy. You get so caught up in the details of everything that is going on around you and that means you sometimes fail to see the full picture. You are working too hard, Matthew. I want you to work less, but accomplish more.

I know. You're probably sighing now and mumbling to yourself about this crazy old man who keeps writing you letters. That's all right. You mumbled and grumbled about me even in your school days. I'm used to it.

What I'm talking about here is the huge difference a small percentage increase can make. I know nothing about your occupation, so we'll use some simple math to illustrate what I'm talking about. Let's assume that we can divide your work into five distinct areas. We'll also assume that you have a rating of 1.5 out of 5 in each area. We can illustrate that easily:

$$1.5 \times 1.5 \times 1.5 \times 1.5 \times 1.5 = 7.6$$

Let's assume that you managed to increase your ranking in each area to 2 out of 5. It now looks like this:

$$2 \times 2 \times 2 \times 2 \times 2 = 32$$

By increasing your overall efficiency in each area, you can increase your total productivity by more than 400 percent! Now what if you increased to 2.5 in each area. That totals 97. What say you actually doubled your output and reached 3 out of 5 in each area. What does that total? 243.

Of course, I'm a teacher, so I have my own personal bias on this. If you make learning a lifelong process, you will steadily improve in every area as you go through life. Think what that can do to your total productivity.

Take a step back, and look at what you are currently doing. See what improvements you can make, and then reap the rewards.

I know it's not easy. We all get crushed down beneath all the things we have to do. It's a matter of deliberately observing what you are doing now and thinking of ways to simplify it, or make it better.

Remember, Matthew, work should be fun. If you enjoy what you're doing, you'll leap out of bed looking forward to the new day. Of course, no job is fun all the time. There are ups and downs in everything. If your work is not fun, or has ceased to be fun, you need to do something about it. See if you can put the pleasure and enjoyment back into your work. If that's not possible, find a new opportunity for yourself. You help no one by stagnating in a position that you no longer love. Remember what I said earlier about finding your passion and then never needing to "work" again? Find your passion, and work becomes fun.

Years ago, someone asked me if I'd carry on teaching if I won a huge lottery. I couldn't understand the question. Why would I give up something I loved doing, just because I had money in the bank? You see, teaching was, and still is, my passion. Tell me, Matthew, if you won Lotto, would you carry on doing what you're doing now?

Think about these things.

Franklin

After dinner, Matthew went for a long walk to think about Mr. Nevin's latest letter. Would he give up his job if he won Lotto? Probably. And how could he step back and watch what he was doing, when there was so much pressure all the time? Of course, he could see what Mr. Nevin was driving at. Increase productivity, and obviously changes would occur. What if the entire sales staff increased their productivity, by say, 10 percent, as well?

A few calculations showed that this would more than make up for the loss of the Lochiel account. Naturally, not everyone would increase sales by 10 percent, but all it needed was a few percent for major changes to occur. A simple change in attitude would be sufficient to achieve that. By the time he returned home, Matthew had an idea.

"Nurture others."

"Find something to believe in."

"A small increase makes a large difference."

"Learning is a lifelong process."

Dear Matthew

Chapter Seven

$\mathcal{M}$ATTHEW BEGAN by discussing his idea with Wilbur and enlisting his support. Mr. Bellowes was quick to agree when Wilbur put it to him. Rather than hold a sales meeting, Wilbur and Matthew spoke to all the reps individually.

Duncan was the last person they spoke to. Rather than discuss it at work, Wilbur and Matthew took him to a small cafe nearby.

"You mean to say," Duncan said, "that if I increase sales 10 percent this month, Brazier will pay for Monica and I to go out for dinner?"

"Correct."

The smile slowly left Duncan's face. "It's impossible for me. Without the Lochiel order my sales are dismal."

"We are basing this on a 10-percent improvement over your last month's total, not including Lochiel. You have just as much a chance as everyone else."

Duncan nodded, but the smile did not return. "You're only doing this because of the Lochiel disaster. That means everyone has to work harder because of me."

"Maybe. But there's a carrot at the end of the stick. I'm not asking anyone to work harder. All I'm saying is, if they increase sales by 10 percent, they'll be rewarded for it."

Duncan sipped his cappuccino as he thought about it. "Okay. That's the first month. What about the following two months?"

"We're looking for a further 10-percent increase. Anyone who achieves that will have a weekend in New York, with tickets to a show. If anyone succeeds in doing it yet again, on the third month, they'll win a week's vacation in Hawaii."

Duncan licked his lips. "Okay. I'll give it my best shot. But what about the rest of the team? This rewards the sales staff, but everyone else will have to work harder, too, and they're not being rewarded."

Matthew reached across the table and patted Duncan's arm. "I'm glad you raised that. No one else even mentioned it."

Wilbur cleared his throat. "Mr. Bellowes and I discussed that. We can't do anything for the first couple of months. But everyone will be rewarded on the third month. What we do depends on the results of this promotion. I promise you that Mr. Bellowes will be generous."

Duncan nodded slowly. "Okay. And if we succeed in this, will Brazier's turnover be back to where it was?"

"It will be better," Wilbur told him. "Much better. Oh, and there's one other thing."

"What's that?"

"You said you'd give it your 'best shot.' That's like saying you'll try. I don't want you to try. I want you to do it. Okay?"

The new initiative created ripples of excitement around the company. People spoke more positively about the future, and Matthew noticed people smiling and laughing again. *Or am I finally seeing their souls?* he wondered.

Even Jennie noticed the increased optimism in Matthew's voice when he phoned on Thursday night.

"Have you been drinking?" she asked.

Matthew laughed. "I'll tell you all about it when I see you," he said. "How are the boys?"

Lying in bed, waiting for sleep, he decided to drive up to his in-law's farm after work the next day. If he left early, he could take a small detour and see how Bernie Nevin was getting on. This wasn't necessary, as Sam and Bernie arrived back at the office shortly after three.

Sam spoke highly of Bernie's ability, and held up a large sheaf of orders as evidence.

"I'm glad he's my replacement," he said. "Most of my customers are friends, and I wanted someone good to look after them once I'm gone."

Matthew had to go home to pack some clothes before heading north. There was another letter from Mr. Nevin in the mailbox. Matthew folded it carefully and placed it in his shirt pocket, planning to read it when he stopped for a meal.

The freeway was jammed. He smiled as he slowly passed the office building he had stopped at a week before, after settling Bernie into his territory. The lights were on, just as they had been before. Tom Gozinski was still hard at work. Matthew snapped his fingers in annoyance, as he had failed to mention this potential client to Bernie. Maybe he should call again, particularly as the traffic was still slow. He looked at his watch. As the family did not know he was coming, perhaps he could stop briefly and have a meal before continuing.

He asked his body if he should stop, and a feeling of calmness and confidence swept through him.

Tom jumped out of his chair when Matthew gently tapped on the window. He grinned when he saw Matthew, and went to let him in.

"You're unbelievable," he told Matthew. "How many sales reps are calling on customers at this time on a Friday night?"

Matthew looked at his watch and apologized for calling so late. "How about you and I have something to eat," he suggested. "You'd probably benefit from half an hour out of your office, and I'm going to eat anyway."

They went to a small restaurant where Tom was well-known. They were given a booth at the back, and Matthew took Tom's advice on what to order. He asked Tom about his family and outside interests, and enjoyed the enthusiasm in Tom's voice as he talked about his children and what they were doing. He confessed to Tom that he was on his way to spend the weekend with his family.

"All the same, you stopped to see me. That was well beyond the call of duty. You'd probably be there by now, instead of listening to me. I'll do the decent thing and keep quiet. Tell me what Brazier has to offer."

It was almost eleven by the time Matthew reached the farmhouse. Everyone was in bed, and Matthew tossed gravel at Jennie's window to attract her attention.

She giggled as she let him in. "This is like being a teenager again!"

Matthew held her close. "How about we pretend we're teenagers for a while."

They sat in the kitchen drinking hot chocolate and catching up on each other's news. It was only when Matthew started telling Jennie about Mr. Nevin's letters that he remembered the unopened one in his pocket. He carefully opened it and read it aloud.

Dear Matthew,
Yes, it's me again. I hope your attitude and approach to life is changing. I know it will be if you're following my suggestions. How do I know they work? Let's just say that many years ago I went through a difficult time and was helped enormously by someone who gave

these ideas to me. They'd been given to him many years before. It feels good to be part of a long tradition, and I have been quietly telling others about these secrets when I felt they needed to hear them. That makes me just one link in a long chain. You are now another link, and I hope that one day you'll extend the chain by at least one more link.

I think you're ready for another lesson from this old teacher. Today I want to talk about planning for the future. I'm not talking about retirement, although I hope you're planning for that as well. I'm talking about a goal that you are working towards. Once you have your goal, your target if you wish, you know where you're headed. I think it was Carlyle who said: "The man without a purpose is like a ship without a rudder; a waif; a nothing; a no man." You need a purpose to keep on track. Mr. Stokes, the school janitor, had a purpose. It was to have the cleanest, tidiest school in the nation. I don't know if he achieved this goal, but even if he didn't, he must have gotten pretty close. It gave dignity, meaning, and purpose to his life. My purpose was to be an excellent teacher.

What is your purpose, Matthew? At one time your purpose was to become a great salesman, just like your dad. Is that still your purpose? If not, spend time finding a new purpose. Here's a small clue—become as good as you possibly can be at whatever job you are doing. That way you'll stand out from the crowd. You'll be noticed, respected, and admired. Of course, there will be small people who'll try to drag you down to their level. There are always plenty of people like that. But you'll be too busy, too focused, too far above them, to even notice.

Mr. Carlyle had much to say about finding your purpose. I particularly like these words: "A man with a half-volition goes backwards and forwards and makes no way on the smoothest road; a man with a whole volition advances on the roughest and will reach his purpose, if there be even a little wisdom in it."

There are countless benefits to having a purpose. The most important is that when you know what you're aiming at, you usually achieve it. Another benefit is that you'll generate more enthusiasm and energy than you could ever imagine possible. That enthusiasm and energy will drive you on to ever-increasing success. When you have a purpose, your health and vitality improve. You'll have a reason to get out of bed in the morning. You'll remain mentally young and vital, no matter how old you may be in physical years. You'll lead a life full of interest, fun, joy, and excitement. Am I exaggerating? I don't think so. Combine your purpose with your passion and you can achieve anything you set your mind on.

That's probably enough for now, Matthew. Just one last thought. When you start doing these things, you are going to have an enormous influence on others; in fact, on everyone whose life touches yours. Your children, for instance, watch and listen and learn every second they're awake. They're busy modeling themselves on you right now. Give them a father they can look up to and be proud of. Wouldn't it be wonderful if they thought to themselves, "One day I'm going to be like him?" Did you perchance think those thoughts when you were young, Matthew?

Yours purposefully,
Franklin

There was a long silence when Matthew finished reading the letter. His eyes felt moist and a tear slid down his cheek as Jennie gently took his hand in hers.

"What an amazing man," she said. Her voice had a quaver in it. "He's speaking to all of us."

Matthew nodded and kissed her neck. Jennie smiled and playfully pushed him away. "Not so fast, darling. I want to hear you read it again first."

Dear Matthew

Chapter Eight

*T*HE FOLLOWING two weeks were hectic, both at home and at work. Summer vacation was over, and the boys were back at school. Sometimes Matthew and Jennie felt that they were simply drivers, taking the boys to and from their various interests.

Sam left, and Matthew spent several days on the road with Bernie. Bernie was determined to increase the sales figures by the required 10 percent to win the dinner, and he worked long hours, calling on existing clients and trying to find new ones. On every visit Matthew was impressed with his energy and capabilities.

One afternoon, Matthew took Bernie to meet Tom Gozinski.

"You mean you call on people during the day, as well as at night?" Tom laughed.

He took them to a nearby coffee shop, and they discussed baseball and sipped coffee. Tom refused to talk business, but accepted Bernie's card as they left.

"I'll be in touch," he said.

It had been exactly two weeks since he had received a letter from Mr. Nevin, Matthew thought as he drove home. He hoped the old man was well. He kept intending to ask Bernie for his distant relative's address, and resolved to do it the next day.

Jason and Eric were at the front gate waiting for him when he arrived home.

"Your letter's arrived," they called out as he drove into the garage.

Jennie and the boys sat down around the dining table and watched Matthew open the envelope. As usual, both sides of the single sheet of paper were covered in beautiful handwriting. Matthew read the letter aloud.

Dear Matthew,

You will be wondering what's happened to me. A spate of letters and then nothing. I've been rather busy lately, but it's given me time to think and there are a couple of matters I want to mention today. I'm sure you know both of these already, but sometimes it doesn't hurt to hear them again. Maybe my slant on them will be a little bit different. If not, please bear with me, as they are important, and build on what we've already discussed.

First of all, stay on top of your thoughts. I know you believe in positive thinking, and that your thoughts can change your life. I imagine you also use positive affirmations. This makes a good start, but there is more to it than that. Often, we get so involved in what we are doing that we forget to say our affirmations. Maybe we have a bad day, and start thinking negative thoughts. Even while thinking those thoughts, we know we are thinking negatively, but because the day has been bad, we keep on thinking that way.

Fortunately, there are things you can do. Have you heard of silent affirmations, Matthew? The Chinese invented these thousands of years ago to motivate and inspire the people. They would use one thing to symbolize something else. For instance, they relate water to money. A fountain outside a building is a silent affirmation of wealth and abundance.

If you like, you could deliberately choose something to represent something else, but I have an idea that is easier to implement. Write down your favorite affirmations and place them somewhere where you will see them regularly. The bathroom, for instance, is a good place. I also have a few affirmations on cards that I keep in my pocket. Whenever I go to my pocket for any reason I pull one out and read it. You can also deliberately take out affirmations from your pocket to read any time you have to wait somewhere. That makes practical use of your waiting time.

You have young children, Matthew. Ask them to draw or paint pictures to represent your favorite affirmations. It might be a good way to introduce them to affirmations. Alternatively, you might draw or paint a picture yourself to represent an affirmation. It does you good to use the creative side of your brain, and—who knows—you might have an unknown talent just waiting to be expressed. Once you have your picture, display it somewhere and it instantly becomes a silent affirmation. Every time you see it, it will bring the affirmation into your mind.

You might find it helpful to imagine yourself acting in a situation in exactly the way your affirmations say you will act. You may think this is simply idle daydreaming. In fact, role-playing of this sort is extremely beneficial. Your subconscious mind cannot tell the difference between imagining something and experiencing it. Doing this will make it that much easier for you to reach your goals.

I said there were two things I wanted to discuss. The second one is to always follow the Golden Rule. Do unto others as you would have them do unto you. When you think about it, this is the only sensible way to get through life. It gives you integrity. It means that you can sleep easily in bed at night. It gives you confidence, self-assurance, and peace of mind. It means you do your best in every situation. It means you will not be haunted by fears, worries, and regrets, because you will have done your best. It means that you are honest, and that is a rare commodity. Do you remember *Hamlet* from your schooldays? In that play Shakespeare wrote: "To be honest, as this world goes, is to be one man picked out of ten thousand."

If you give your children nothing more, teach them the Golden Rule. It will ensure that they lead good, worthwhile, rewarding lives. They will be respected, admired, trusted, and sought out by others. They will have integrity. What could be more important than that?

Your friend,

Franklin

When he finished, Matthew put the sheet of paper down and looked at Jennie.

"That's beautiful," she said. "It's warm, and so wise. It's almost like hearing from your guardian angel."

Matthew stood up and put his arms around her. The boys quickly joined in.

For the next two weeks Matthew spoke to Bernie almost every day. Although he intended to ask him for Mr. Nevin's address, he never thought of it during their conversations.

Everyone paid close attention to the sales figures as the end of the month drew near. Duncan showed the greatest percentage increase, probably caused by his guilt over losing the Lochiel account. Although he never mentioned it, Matthew heard that Duncan was visiting Lochiel every few days, in an attempt to get the business back. Four of the other sales reps had recorded increases of more than 10 percent. Matthew's sales showed an increase of several percent. He ruefully told himself that if he had spent less time helping Bernie, he would have reached the target.

By the twenty-seventh of the month, Bernie had an 8-percent increase over his predecessor's figures, although part of this had been brought in by Sam before he had left. Surprisingly, Mr. Bellowes felt that Bernie should be given the reward.

"He's new. He's doing well. Let's reward him."

Wilbur frowned and shook his head. Normally, he was in favor of anything that helped keep the sales force motivated. However, this time he disagreed.

"Everyone knows the rules," he said. "We insisted on a 10-percent increase. Of course, I want Bernie to win the night out. But he must increase sales by 10 percent."

The following day, Matthew drove north to spend the day with Bernie. They called on the customers together, and Bernie received several small orders. Most of the people they called on promised him an order on the first of the month. Bernie was philosophical about not gaining a 10-percent increase.

"There are three factors," he said, holding up three fingers. He tapped each one in turn as he spoke. "It's my first month on the job. None of the clients know me, so they're probably being cautious. Finally, I've wasted quite a bit of time trying to find some of the accounts. Next month will be easier."

"You still have two days," Matthew told him. "It's an outside chance, I know, but you may yet do it."

In his heart, Matthew knew it was unlikely. It was getting dark when Matthew began the long drive home. He had not realized how late it was. Traffic on the freeway was also a problem. The traffic slowed to a crawl as he passed Tom Gozinski's premises. As always, the lights were on.

Almost by habit, Matthew left the freeway. Soon he was knocking on Tom's window.

"It's great that you're here," Tom greeted him. "I want to give you an order."

"Thanks," Matthew said. "I'll ask Bernie to pick it up tomorrow."

Tom shook his head. "It's only tiny, and I need it in a hurry. Don't worry about it. I'll get it locally."

Matthew laughed. "You will not! I'll take the order and we'll get it to you by lunchtime at the latest."

The order was for less than fifty dollars. "There'll be more," Tom said, almost apologetically. "But that's all I need right now." He looked at his watch. "I'm about ready to eat. Are you hungry?"

Matthew dropped the boys off at school on his way to work the next morning. He went to the warehouse on the way to his office and asked the supervisor to make sure that Tom's order went out right away. He checked an hour later and found that it had been sent. At lunchtime, he called Tom Gozinski's secretary and learned that the order had arrived.

He spent the afternoon phoning his regular customers to see if they needed anything urgently. Wilbur strolled into the sales office at four-thirty, smiling broadly.

"Thanks, everyone," he said, looking around the room. "Largely thanks to the promotion, sales have been almost as good as last month. You've shown that Brazier can survive perfectly well without the Lochiel account." He went round the room formally shaking hands with everyone.

"And we've one day to go," he said, just before he returned to his own office. "We might yet equal last month."

There was another letter from Mr. Nevin waiting for Matthew when he arrived home. He caressed it and placed it on the dining room table.

"Dinner isn't ready yet," Matthew told his boys. "How about we have a game of soccer?"

Jennie called them in half an hour later. Hot, exhausted, and happy, they sat down around the table.

"Open your letter," Jason said.

Matthew picked it up and turned it over and over in his hand. "Later," he said. "After dinner."

Was it his imagination, he thought as they enjoyed the meal, *or were they all getting along much better than they used to?* He gazed fondly at the boys as they played a game of listing the capital cities of different countries around the world. He caught Jennie's eye and they exchanged a smile.

"Good day?" she asked.

Matthew nodded. "It was, actually. But this is the best part, right now."

He did not open the envelope until the children had gone to bed. Jennie sat down on the couch beside him, and they read it together.

Dear Matthew,
This is my last letter to you. Don't feel sad about this. I'm the one who should be feeling sad, but I've given you more than enough to work on. In fact, if you master even a small fraction of what I've suggested, you'll be extremely successful.

Be successful in your own way, Matthew. Never try to live other people's hopes or dreams. You cannot find peace of mind or happiness that way. And don't do anything solely to win the approval of others. Be true to yourself and make your life an exciting adventure.

Be positive. Every morning, when you get out of bed, you have the power to make it a good day or a bad day, simply by choosing your thoughts. Choose positive thoughts and every day will be a good day. Naturally, some will be better than others, but you can make every day a good one. No matter what happens in your life, you can be happy, if you want to be. Be happy, Matthew. It makes a huge difference, not only to you, but to everyone who is associated with you. Happiness is simply a habit. Make someone else happy, and you'll become happier yourself.

Do the things that need to be done. Don't seek praise from others—you don't always get it. Often, your best efforts will be ignored by others. That doesn't matter, as long as you know that you've done the very best you can.

I have enormous faith in you, Matthew. Maybe even more than you have in yourself. You can make a difference in this world, if you want to. I've tried to do exactly that, in my own way.

These simple principles are universal. They are so old that everyone should know all about them. In my experience, hardly anyone has heard of them. You could almost say they were secrets—success secrets. Look at the lives of the greatest people throughout history and you'll find that they used these principles, consciously or unconsciously. Study them carefully, Matthew, and then make good use of them.

I'm now passing the mantle on to you. As I told you before, someone handed it to me many, many years ago. In doing this, I'm confident that one day you'll do the same thing for someone else.

Please think kindly of me, Matthew.

Love to you all,

Franklin

Jennie drew Matthew nearer to her and kissed him tenderly.

"I'm grateful to him, too," she said. "Mr. Nevin has brought us all so much closer. His letters were for all of us."

"I've got to find him," Matthew said. "He's done so much for me. I have to thank him."

The last day of the month was unusually hectic. The sales staff were all busy trying to gain a few more orders to ensure they won the weekend away.

Shortly after lunch, Bernie arrived. He raced into Matthew's office and showed him an order.

"I think I'm up 10 percent, after all," he said.

Matthew looked at the order. It was a $3,000 order from Tom Gozinski's corporation.

"That's fantastic!" he exclaimed. "Well done!"

Bernie shook his head. "It's not really my order. It's yours. Tom told me all about your evening visits to him. He also said that the trial order he gave you arrived in record time. So this is your order."

"Nonsense," Matthew said. "Tom's in your territory. He's your client." He looked at the order again. "He has a good business. You never know, he might yet become a replacement for the Lochiel account."

"Just one thing," Bernie said. "Why did he give me the order today? If I'd been him, I'd have placed it on the first of the month. Does he know about the competition?"

Matthew shrugged his shoulders. "We might have discussed it. I'm not sure." He smiled at the new rep. "You've had an incredible first month, Bernie. Keep up the great work." As Bernie turned to go, Matthew asked him for Franklin B. Nevin's address.

"Use affirmations."

"Do unto others as you would have them do unto you."

"Be successful in your own way."

"Choose your thoughts."

"Make a difference."

Dear Matthew

Chapter Nine

WILBUR APPEARED at the door of the sales office at four that afternoon and silently beckoned to Matthew. Puzzled, Matthew got up and followed him back to his office.

"What's the problem?" he asked.

Wilbur answered the question by handing him a sheet of paper. It listed the salespeople who had achieved a 10-percent increase during the month. Matthew's name was not on the list.

"You're only a few hundred dollars short," Wilbur said. "Who can you think of who'll give you an order at four o'clock on the last day of the month?"

Matthew laughed. "I've contacted everyone. I could put pressure on a few people and ask for a favor, but I'm not prepared to do that. Thanks, Wilbur. I appreciate you telling me, but it's not meant to be."

"But it was you who suggested the competition."

Matthew shook his head. "That's got nothing to do with it. I didn't increase my sales enough to win."

"You gave up several days to help Bernie."

"That was my decision, and I enjoyed it. Thanks, Wilbur. I'll try again next month."

He realized that he'd used the word "try" as he returned to the sales office.

Matthew sat at his desk and looked around the room at the other salespeople, all discussing the competition. The room was full of cheerful sounds as the sales team relaxed and unwound after a hectic month. Several of them already knew that they'd achieved their targets, but others were not so certain. It was good to see that Bernie was already an accepted member of the team, and had achieved his target, thanks to Tom Gozinski.

On an impulse, Matthew phoned Tom to thank him for giving Bernie the order.

"Are you all right?" Tom said. "You don't sound your usual self."

Matthew forced himself to laugh. "I've never been better. Brazier reached their sales target for the month, and I'm especially thrilled that Bernie made it, and that's thanks to you."

Tom chuckled. "I remember you mentioning it, and it seemed like a fun thing to do." There was a brief pause. "How about you, Matthew? Did you reach your target?"

"'Fraid not, but I'll have another go next month."

"No, no. That's not right." Tom sounded concerned. "I've never had anyone call on me the way you have. You should be at the top of the list. Tell me again, what area does your territory cover?"

Five minutes later, Matthew was in his car fighting Friday afternoon traffic. It was a crazy idea to make a cold call at this time of day, but Tom had insisted he do it. Who would give a complete stranger an order for hundreds of dollars on the last day of the month? Think positive, Matthew told himself. While waiting for the light to turn green, Matthew asked his body if it was a good idea to proceed. To his surprise, he experienced a feeling of enthusiasm and energy. Smiling now, he finished the drive without stress, and parked in the lot just before five.

The receptionist was putting on her coat when Matthew walked in.

"Could I see Josh McCormick, please," Matthew said, and handed over his card.

"He may already have left," the woman said doubtfully. "I'll try his extension." A moment later, she handed the phone to Matthew. "He's in."

Matthew briefly explained who he was and why he was calling, and, to his surprise, Josh said he'd come out to see him.

Several minutes passed before a tall, athletic-looking man in his late twenties bounced into the lobby.

"Hi," he said. "I'm Josh McCormick."

After they had shaken hands, Josh sat down and said, "Who put you up to this?"

"What do you mean?"

"This must be a joke, right? I know about Brazier, but you've never called on us before, as far as I know. Now you turn up just as we're closing. Tell me it's a joke."

Matthew shook his head. "It's no joke. A friend of mine, Tom Gozinski—"

"Tom Gozinski?" Josh leapt to his feet. "Come through to my office."

On the way, Josh explained that Tom Gozinski had been president of the corporation for some years, before leaving to start up his own business. "He employed me," Josh said. "I owe him a great deal, so I'm happy to see what you have to offer."

Thirty minutes later, Matthew left with an order.

On his way home, Matthew called Tom on his cell phone to thank him.

"You're sure you didn't speak to Josh before I got there?" he asked.

"I was going to, but when you insisted that I didn't, I kept my word. So he gave you an order?"

"Yes, thank you very much. More than large enough to qualify me for the dinner."

"Good. I'm pleased to hear it. You're a great salesman, Matthew, and if you ever feel like a change of scene, make sure you speak to me first."

"Thank you so much, Tom. And thank you very much for the order, also."

"That wasn't my doing. You got the order. Goodnight!"

That evening, Matthew took his family out for dinner to celebrate. While waiting for dessert, Jason and Eric handed him a card they had made. On the front was a picture of a salesman, complete with briefcase, but with the addition of a cape. The salesman was flying above the clouds intent on reaching his next customer. Above the picture the boys had written "To a great salesman." Inside, it read "For dad, our favorite salesman. You're Number One! Love from Jason and Eric."

Tears came to Matthew's eyes as he gazed at the card.

"Thank you so much, boys," he said. "What a wonderful surprise. How did you know I'd succeeded in the competition?"

"Because you're Number One!" Eric said.

"Number One with us," Jason added.

In bed that night, Matthew held Jennie close. "That was so nice of the kids," he said. "I really appreciated getting that card. It'll be going to work with me tomorrow." He paused. "And I so appreciate their faith in me. They knew I was going to succeed."

Jennie giggled. "I wasn't going to tell you this, but maybe I should. That card was to cheer you up when you got home tonight. We thought you'd put so much time into helping Bernie that you had no chance of reaching your target. Succeeding made it even better."

"Do you think I spent too much time helping Bernie?"

"No, of course not. I think Mr. Nevin is probably extremely grateful that you helped his young relative."

"It wasn't because he's related to Franklin. I'd have done that for anyone."

"And that's why I married you, honey. You don't always say much, but deep down you're a kind, caring person."

Matthew kissed her tenderly. He laughed. "Let's be teenagers again."

Chapter Ten

*I*T WAS Saturday morning again. Matthew and Jennie sat in the shade of their back porch and watched the boys kicking their soccer ball back and forth.

"Are you sure you don't want to come?" Matthew asked.

Jennie smiled and nodded her head. "I'd love to meet your Mr. Nevin, but I think the first time you should go on your own. We'll be waiting to hear all about it when you get back."

"Okay." Matthew leaned over and kissed her, and then called out a cheerful goodbye to the boys.

It was strange how things worked out, he mused to himself as he drove down the freeway. Mr. Nevin had been deliberately mysterious. His letters had never contained a return address, so theoretically he could have lived anywhere in the country. However, his letters had also never been postmarked, so it was probably not surprising that Mr. Nevin lived only a few miles away.

Mind you, he was obviously an extremely private man. There was no indication of his existence in phone books, on the Internet, or anywhere else. If it hadn't been for Bernie Nevin, Matthew would never have tracked him down.

Mr. Nevin's street was a quiet, tree-shaded cul de sac. His house, a two-level timber house, gleaming with fresh paint, was near the end, slightly raised above the road. The front yard was neat and well tended. Flower beds adorned both sides of the path leading to the front door.

Matthew parked outside, and took a few deep breaths before picking up his gift and getting out. It was a beautifully bound edition of Richard Hakluyt's *Voyages*, which Matthew had found in an antiquarian bookstore. Mr. Nevin loved the Tudor period, and Matthew was certain he'd be thrilled to receive such a magnificent gift. He fondled the package, wondering if it might embarrass Mr. Nevin to be given such a valuable present. Matthew shook his head. It was too late to worry about that now.

He got out of the car and looked up at the house. Several windows were open. Hopefully, Mr. Nevin was home. He walked slowly up the path and rang the bell.

For a moment there was no sound from inside, but then a woman's voice called out, "I'll be right with you." He heard her coming down the stairs, and then the front door opened a few inches, held by a safety chain.

"Yes?" she inquired.

Matthew smiled. "Sorry to bother you," he said. "I'm looking for Mr. Nevin."

"He's at work. He won't be back till after five."

"No, no. I was wanting Mr. Franklin Nevin. I'm sure he's retired."

The door partially closed and then opened wide. He found himself looking at a small, round woman with a quizzical look on her face. She was wearing a smiley-face apron over a floral dress.

"Franklin?" she asked. "Franklin?" She frowned and looked earnestly at Matthew. "Franklin's dead. We buried him five years ago."

"But I've brought him a present," Matthew said, realizing how stupid the words sounded as he spoke them. "He wrote me some letters, and I wanted to thank him. I'm obviously too late. Much too late."

The woman reached out and patted his arm. "Franklin was a good man. He helped many people. You're part of his legacy to the world." She sighed heavily. "We all miss him." She smiled at Matthew. "Come inside. You look as if you need a cup of coffee."

An hour later, Matthew thanked her and returned to his car. He carefully placed the photograph she had given him on the passenger seat, and waved to Mr. Nevin's daughter-in-law before heading home.

Jennie came into the garage before he got out of the car.

"Did you see him?" she asked.

Matthew nodded. He held up the photograph. "Here he is. I told him I'm a great salesman, just like my dad." Matthew looked at the smiling face in the frame. "But just between you and me, Mr. Nevin, you are the greatest salesman I've ever known."

Dear Matthew

Afterword

$\mathcal{M}$ANY YEARS ago I sat down to write a letter to a friend who was going through a difficult time in his life. Instead of the letter I intended to write, a story emerged that was ultimately published as *Seven Secrets to Success*. I have received more letters from readers of that book than from all my other books put together. This small book has also been translated into nine other languages, showing that its message is universal in scope.

Ever since *Seven Secrets to Success* was published in 1997, people have been asking me for a sequel. At first I thought this would be an easy task, but it proved much harder than I anticipated. This is because in many ways I did not write *Seven Secrets to Success;* the book wrote itself when I sat down to write the letter to my friend. There was no forward planning, plotting, or outlining on my part. Consequently, when I sat down to consciously write a sequel, everything I came up with seemed contrived.

More recently, I was on my way to a meeting with a group of friends, one of whom had been pushing me to write "another *Seven Secrets.*" I was planning to tell her that there would be no sequel, after all. I was caught in a traffic jam on the freeway, and suddenly the complete story of *Success Secrets: Letters to Matthew* came to me. I must have been poor company that night, because all I wanted to do was return home and start work on this book.

As Franklin B. Nevin died five years before the incidents retold in this book, where did the letters come from? There is an interesting phenomenon known as automatic writing, in which people hold a pen and produce words without any conscious thought or effort. Alfred Lord Tennyson, William Butler Yeats, and Gertrude Stein are just a few of the many authors who experimented with automatic writing. Many books have been written in this way, including *Swan on a Black Sea* by Geraldine Cummins.* C. H. Broad, the famous British philosopher, wrote in his preface

* Published by Routledge and Kegan Paul in London, England, 1965.

to this book: "There is, undoubtedly, some independent evidence for the existence, in some few persons, of remarkable creative and dramatizing powers, which reveal themselves only when their possessor is in a dissociated state."

Usually, the person is aware that he or she is automatic writing. However, there are instances where the person has no memory of the experience at all. Consequently, it is possible that Matthew was writing the letters himself, but had no conscious memory of doing so.

If this is the case, where did the information come from? It most likely came from Matthew's subconscious mind, which gave him the information he needed to know at a particular time. Alternatively, the material may have come from the universal mind, where all ideas and inspiration come from. Maybe Matthew subconsciously used automatic writing to get in touch with the spirit or soul of Franklin B. Nevin.

Of course, it doesn't really matter where the information came from as long as it proves helpful to you today. Matthew is a salesman. However, the principles that Franklin B. Nevin revealed in his letters can be used by anyone, no matter what field he or she may be in.

I hope that you will implant them in your own mind, and become "successful in your own way."

☾ REACH FOR THE MOON

Llewellyn publishes hundreds of books on your favorite subjects! To get these exciting books, including the ones on the following pages, check your local bookstore or order them directly from Llewellyn.

ORDER BY PHONE

- Call toll-free within the U.S. and Canada, 1-800-THE MOON
- In Minnesota, call (651) 291-1970
- We accept VISA, MasterCard, and American Express

ORDER BY MAIL

- Send the full price of your order (MN residents add 7% sales tax) in U.S. funds, plus postage & handling to:

  Llewellyn Worldwide
  P.O. Box 64383, Dept. 1-56718-788-9
  St. Paul, MN 55164-0383, U.S.A.

Postage & Handling

- **Standard** (U.S., Mexico, & Canada)

If your order is:

  $20.00 or under, add $5.00

  $20.01–$100.00, add $6.00

  Over $100, shipping is free

(Continental U.S. orders ship UPS. AK, HI, PR, & P.O. Boxes ship USPS 1st class. Mex. & Can. ship PMB.)

- **Second Day Air** (Continental U.S. only): $10.00 for one book + $1.00 per each additional book
- **Express** (AK, HI, & PR only) [Not available for P.O. Box delivery. For street address delivery only.]: $15.00 for one book + $1.00 per each additional book
- **International Surface Mail:** Add $1.00 per item
- **International Airmail:** Books—Add the retail price of each item; Non-book items—Add $5.00 per item

  Please allow 4–6 weeks for delivery on all orders.
  Postage and handling rates subject to change.

Discounts

We offer a 20% discount to group leaders or agents. You must order a minimum of 5 copies of the same book to get our special quantity price.

FREE CATALOG

Get a free copy of our color catalog, *New Worlds of Mind and Spirit*. Subscribe for just $10.00 in the United States and Canada ($30.00 overseas, airmail). Many bookstores carry *New Worlds*—ask for it!

Visit our web site at www.llewellyn.com for more information.

***Seven Secrets
to Success***

A Story of Hope

Richard Webster

Originally written as a letter from the author to his suicidal friend, this inspiring little book has been photocopied, passed along from person to person, and even appeared on the Internet without the author's permission. Now available in book form, this underground classic offers hope to the weary and motivation for us all to let go of the past and follow our dreams.

It is the story of Kevin, who at the age of twenty-eight is on the verge of suicide after the failure of his business and his marriage. Then he meets Todd Melvin, an elderly gentleman with a mysterious past. As their friendship unfolds, Todd teaches Kevin seven secrets—secrets that can give you the power to turn your life around, begin anew, and reap success beyond your wildest dreams.

1-56718-797-8, 144 pp., 5³⁄₁₆ x 8   **$6.95**

To order, call 1-800-THE MOON
Prices subject to change without notice

Soul Mates
Understanding
Relationships Across Time

Richard Webster

The eternal question: how do you find your soul mate—that special, magical person with whom you have spent many previous incarnations? Popular metaphysical author Richard Webster explores every aspect of the soul mate phenomenon in his newest release.

The incredible soul mate connection allows you and your partner to progress even further with your souls' growth and development with each incarnation. *Soul Mates* begins by explaining reincarnation, karma, and the soul, and prepares you to attract your soul mate to you. After reading examples of soul mates from the author's own practice, and famous soul mates from history, you will learn how to recall your past lives. In addition, you will gain valuable tips on how to strengthen your relationship so it grows stronger and better as time goes by.

1-56718-789-7, 216 pp., 5³⁄₁₆ x 8   **$12.95**

Spirit Guides & Angel Guardians
Contact Your Invisible Helpers

Richard Webster

They come to our aid when we least expect it, and they disappear as soon as their work is done. Invisible helpers are available to all of us; in fact, we all regularly receive messages from our guardian angels and spirit guides but usually fail to recognize them. This book will help you to realize when this occurs. And when you carry out the exercises provided, you will be able to communicate freely with both your guardian angels and spirit guides.

You will see your spiritual and personal growth take a huge leap forward as soon as you welcome your angels and guides into your life. This book contains numerous case studies that show how angels have touched the lives of others, just like yourself. Experience more fun, happiness, and fulfillment than ever before. Other people will also notice the difference as you become calmer, more relaxed, and more loving than ever before.

1-56718-795-1, 368 pp., 5³/₁₆ x 8   **$9.95**

101 Feng Shui Tips
for the Home

Richard Webster

101
FENG SHUI
TIPS
for
the
Home

RICHARD
WEBSTER

For thousand of years, people in the Far East have used feng shui to improve their home and family lives and live in harmony with the earth. Certainly, people who practice feng-shui achieve a deep contentment that is denied most others. They usually do well romantically and financially. Architects around the world are beginning to incorporate the concepts of feng shui into their designs. Even people like Donald Trump freely admit to using feng shui.

Now you can make subtle and inexpensive changes to your home that can literally transform your life. If you're in the market for a house, learn what to look for in room design, single level vs. split level, staircases, front door location, and more. If you want to improve upon your existing home, find out how its current design may be creating negative energy, and discover simple ways to remedy the situation without the cost of major renovations or remodeling.

1-56718-809-5, 192 pp., 5³/₁₆ x 8   **$9.95**

Feng Shui
for Beginners
Successful Living by Design

Richard Webster

Not advancing fast enough in your career? Maybe your desk is located in a "negative position." Wish you had a more peaceful family life? Hang a mirror in your dining room and watch what happens. Is money flowing out of your life rather than into it? You may want to look to the construction of your staircase!

For thousands of years, the ancient art of feng shui has helped people harness universal forces and lead lives rich in good health, wealth, and happiness. The basic techniques in *Feng Shui for Beginners* are very simple, and you can put them into place immediately in your home and work environments. Gain peace of mind, a quiet confidence, and turn adversity to your advantage with feng shui remedies.

1-56718-803-6, 240 pp., 5¼ x 8, illus. $12.95

Feng Shui for
Love & Romance

Richard Webster

For thousands of years, the Chinese have known that if they arrange their homes and possessions in the right way, they will attract positive energy into their life, including a life rich in love and friendship. Now you can take advantage of this ancient knowledge so you can attract the right partner to you; if you're currently in a relationship, you can strengthen the bond between you and your beloved.

It's amazingly simple and inexpensive. Want your partner to start listening to you? Display some yellow flowers in the *Ken* (communication) area of your home. Do you want to bring more friends of both sexes into your life? Place some green plants or candles in the *Chien* (friendship) area. Is your relationship good in most respects but lacking passion between the sheets? Be forewarned—once you activate this area with feng shui, you may have problems getting enough sleep at night!

1-56718-792-7, 192 pp., 5¼ x 8   **$9.95**

To order, call 1-800-THE MOON
Prices subject to change without notice

Feng Shui for
Apartment Living

Richard Webster

FENG
SHUI
for
Apartment
Living

RICHARD
WEBSTER

Don't think that just because you live in an apartment complex, an one-room studio, or a tiny dormitory that you can't benefit from the ancient art of feng shui. You can indeed make subtle changes to your living area that will literally transform your life. Those who practice feng shui are noticing marked improvements in all areas—romantic, financial, career, family, health, even fame.

Learn what to look for when selecting an apartment. Find out where your four positive and four negative locations are, and avoid pointing your bed toward the "disaster" location. Discover the best places for other furniture, and how to remedy negative areas with plants, mirrors, crystals, and wind chimes. You will also learn how to conduct a feng shui evaluation for others.

1-56718-794-3, 192 pp., 5¼ x 8, illus.   **$9.95**

To order, call 1-800-THE MOON
Prices subject to change without notice

*Feng Shui for
the Workplace*

Richard Webster

All over the East, business people regularly consult feng shui practitioners because they know it gives them an extra edge for success. Feng shui is the art of living in harmony with the earth. It's about increasing the flow of ch'i in your environment—the universal life force that is found in all living things.

Chances are if you're feeling stuck in your career, your ch'i is also stuck; getting it moving again will benefit you in all areas of your life. Whether you want to increase productivity in your factory, decrease employee turnover in your office, increase sales in your retail store, or bring more customers to your home consulting business, *Feng Shui for the Workplace* offers the tips and solutions for every business scenario. Individual employees can even use this book to decorate their work space for better job satisfaction.

1-56718-808-7, 192 pp., 5³⁄₁₆ x 8, illus.   **$9.95**

*Feng Shui for
Success & Happiness*

Richard Webster

"If you want to be happy," a wise man once said, "be happy!" However, it is not always easy to remain happy when your environment is working against you. Your home should be a place where you can completely be yourself. You should be able to relax there and forget all the cares and problems of the outside world. Consequently, many of your happiest moments should be spent in your home.

The ancient Chinese noticed that different environments had a direct bearing on contentment and even luck. Later on, these factors would become known as feng shui, the art of living in harmony with the earth. Whether you live in a one-room apartment or a sprawling mansion, *Feng Shui for Success & Happiness* will show you how to activate the energy, or ch'i, in your home to improve your environment and to achieve happiness and abundance.

1-56718-815-X, 168 pp., 5¼ x 8, illus.   **$9.95**

***Aura Reading
for Beginners***
*Develop Your
Psychic Awareness for
Health & Success*

Richard Webster

When you lose your temper, don't be surprised if a dirty red haze suddenly appears around you. If you do something magnanimous, your aura will expand. Now you can learn to see the energy that emanates off yourself and other people through the proven methods taught by Richard Webster in his psychic training classes.

Learn to feel the aura, see the colors in it, and interpret what those colors mean. Explore the chakra system, and how to restore balance to chakras that are over- or understimulated. Then you can begin to imprint your desires into your aura to attract what you want in your life.

1-56718-798-6, 208 pp., 5³⁄₁₆ x 8   **$9.95**